Gentlemen And Ladies

BEYOND GRADUATION

How to become the person you have always wanted to be.

By Terrance Buck

Copyright © 2008 Terrance Buck

GBR Publishing
24733 Clayton Road
Grass Valley, California 95949

ISBN: 978-0-578-00118-0

Forward

This book is not intended to be an all-encompassing guide for life. Rather, it is an attempt to give young men and women the advantage of a "heads-up" on many of the hazards of life without having to learn lessons the hard way. Some advice is in the form of familiar clichés that bear explanation. These are "words to live by" that I dearly wish someone would have explained to me in my early years of adulthood. I have gathered them together here for the benefit of my children whom are now coming of age. It is my sincerest hope that you may find this book helpful and can use it to avoid some of the pitfalls that I, and others of my generation, did not.

1) Never talk to one man/woman about romancing another man/woman.

Men should only discuss their female interests with other men and likewise women should only discuss their male interests with other women. Generally speaking, many people are quite empathetic and will listen to your romantic woes with a great interest. Often they will become emotionally involved in your situation. The more you discuss your social life with your confidant of the opposite sex, the closer the two of you will become emotionally. You will bond and begin to look at each other differently. Be aware of the motivations behind this person's advice. While it may seem sound, a woman's advice about how a man should behave must be taken with a grain of salt, and the same holds true for a man's advice about how a woman should act. It may or may not be objective, but it is really only an indication of how they would act in a given situation. Like everyone, male or female, your advisor has his/her own agenda and it will become increasingly slanted toward your becoming his/her mate. Presumably, this is not why you went for advice about your other romantic liaison. Should a dog ask a cat for advice on how to be more dog-like? And if a dog did ask, how much credibility should he attribute to the cat?

2) Never eat muffins or snacks or drink coffee at the beginning of a staff meeting.

Again, a little forethought is in order. Muffins and coffee will have a predictable effect. Presumably, there was a reason for the meeting and you don't want to be forced to miss important announcements or risk offending your supervisor by leaving in the middle for an emergency trip down the hall.

3) Never scrimp on your tools; you'll curse every time you pick them up.

The main reason for purchasing a tool is to make a difficult job easier. Few things are more frustrating than trying to accomplish a task with tools that are weak, of inferior quality, or not shaped correctly. It is always better to have the proper equipment than to spend twice the time and have your blood pressure soar by trying to get by with substandard tools.

4) The right tool for the right job.

A cliché to be sure, but there is a good point here. Your projects will go together smoother and the finished product will look and operate better if you use the correct tools in the assembly/repair. Using a standard screwdriver easily strips Philips head screws. A ball peen hammer will bend nails and damage wood if used in place of a framing hammer. Forcing a pipe into a 45 degree angle because you don't have a 90 degree fitting will cost you a lot more when the pipe cracks than it will cost you to run out to the store for the proper piece.

5) Don't fish off the company pier.

Office romances may seem both convenient and inevitable but they rarely end on a positive note. At the very least, your coworkers will be distracted by your relationship and you will become the subject of much gossip and speculation. There is also the question of how well you and your partner can concentrate in each other's presence. You may want to consider the effect on your relationship if one or the other of you is promoted. Can you maintain a personal relationship as equals with a person whom is your supervisor at work? What will be the effect on office productivity if your fling ends badly? What if after the break up you begin seeing someone else in the office? This sort of drama has no place in the work environment. Guaranteed, an office romance is a sure way to shorten your tenure at a company.

6) Never pass up an opportunity to use the bathroom.

It may delay you a minute or two, but the alternative is to squirm and put up with discomfort, or worse, be forced to leave during a speech, meeting or presentation. It is generally a good idea to plan ahead in order to avoid disrupting the flow of an event. Has arriving at someone's door ever embarrassed you, when the first words you utter after "Hello" are a strained, "May use your bathroom?"

7) Cultivate the habits in private that you wish to display in public.

Anything that you wish to do well must be practiced, and when distracted you will revert to doing what feels natural. If in private you chew on pencils, belch loudly, or pick your nose, then when you are completely focused upon something, or absentmindedly performing an unchallenging task, the chances are very good that you will forget the company you are in and engage in a public behavior that you ordinarily would not. Always act in a gentlemanly or ladylike way. Practice politeness and good hygiene in private settings and you won't have to worry about what may come out when you're not paying attention.

8)   Always let your boss have the first say.

Two office workers and their supervisor are standing at the water cooler one morning when out pops the "Water-Cooler Genie" who offers them one wish each. The first man says, "I wish that I were far away on a tropical island with nothing but sun and surf, plenty to eat and drink, and nothing to do all day but lie in the shade and drink fruit juice." Poof! The man is gone, his wish granted. The second man thinks for a moment and then says, "I wish that I were in a Swiss alpine village high in the Alps, surrounded by beautiful Swiss maidens who feed me wine and cheese all day, and wait on me hand and foot." The Genie waves a hand, there is a puff of smoke, and the second office worker disappears, his wish granted. The Genie looks at the supervisor and asks, "And what is your wish?" After a moment's thought the supervisor says, "I want those two guys back at work after lunch."

9) Never change lanes in an intersection.

People waiting to pullout into traffic are searching for a clear opening and will not be looking at the far lanes but only at the curb lane. Often, they will aggressively lurch into a brief lull between cars and will not even notice you veering into the same opening until you meet.

10) Do not develop bad habits simply because they are convenient and seem to have no impact.

Bad habits are very difficult to break even when they do become inconvenient or dangerous. I know a man who learned to drive in a small town on the Great Plains. At a young age he developed a habit of rolling through stop signs. He would always look both ways but in that part of the country he could see for a mile in any direction. Since he moved to the suburbs of a large city he has been in several accidents because he still does not come to a complete stop and watch for cross traffic. It is important to remember that most rules are in place for a reason. If you give them some thought you may come to realize how much sense they make and how important it is to observe them. Develop good habits early and avoid doing things simply because they are convenient.

11) Never pass up a good thing.

Just be sure that you can objectively identify whether something really is a good thing. Put some thought into the ramifications of your partaking of the "good thing" before you rush in. Many opportunities seem appealing until you look beneath the surface. Often there are hidden consequences. Having said that, don't be afraid to reach out and take hold of an opportunity. Do not let fear of the unknown keep you from taking chances. If you come across a good thing with no strings attached, or at least strings that you can live with, then go for it with gusto!

12) Before considering marriage stop and think, "If I came home and found him/her in bed with someone else, would I be mad enough to hurt them?"

Not just disappointed, hurt, or emotionally distraught, but blind rage angry. If the answer is yes, then realistically, you are probably not in love but in lust. Lust is not a good reason for marriage.

13) Know that there is a marked difference between friends and acquaintances.

Most people know a great many individuals in a passing sense and a smaller number well. Neither of these categories can be considered friends as you and they have not attained the level of intimate knowledge of one another's lives that would prove loyalty and trust. Friends are those people whom you know very well and can count on to back you up in an emergency. Friends may not help you break the law nor even always take your side in an argument, but friends are willing to help whenever they can even if it's inconvenient. A friend will stand by you when you are in trouble. A friend will forgive you for minor transgressions like being late or putting a dent in his/her car. It is not necessary to tell people whether you consider them to be a friend. In fact, that may lead to resentment if they don't make the grade. Just be aware that if you consider someone to be a friend then you have a responsibility to safeguard that relationship. You have a higher level of commitment to that person's well being. Cherish your friends. Most people only make a few true friends during the course of their lives.

14) If your wife or girlfriend asks you, "Does this outfit make me look fat?" The answer is always an emphatic "No."

Note: Resist the temptation to add, "The outfit has nothing to do with it."

15) Regardless of your actual or imagined skill level, read the instructions.

We all like to think that we are smart enough to figure out puzzles without help. In today's world of competition, no one wants to admit they don't know what to do. However, the truly smart people are those who thoroughly read the instructions prior to starting the project. They finish faster and generally end up with a fully functional and attractive finished product. Contrary to popular opinion, when an assembly project is complete you are not supposed to have a few interesting looking pieces left over. Most of us are not design engineers and we may not know why certain parts are important. Presumably they serve a purpose, so read the instructions and install them in the proper configuration.

16) Be early for all appointments.

If being late is unavoidable then call ahead. Essentially, being late is like telling someone that they are not important to you. You may not think that actively as you prepare for an appointment. You may even be thinking that you are simply afraid to go. However, as you think of things that you "simply <u>must</u> do" prior to leaving for the meeting, subconsciously you are categorizing your meeting as being less important than feeling safe and secure. Other people recognize this pattern because we all sometimes feel that way. You will not be fooling anyone with excuses that begin "My wife she…" "My son he…" or "My dog it…" People will begin to realize how little importance they carry in your life and mind. At this point, especially if you are habitually late, they will begin to disregard you and focus upon other more rewarding and predictable relationships.

17) Resist the urge to pursue recreational sex.

A person who is a slave to his/her sex drive will always be lonely no matter how many people he/she spends time with. A sexual relationship <u>can</u> be a wonderfully fulfilling thing. When two people reach a point in their relationship when they want to share the deepest intimacy, physical interactions can be very gratifying. The danger comes in substituting the physical closeness for the emotional bonding. Sex creates an emotional and physiological connection that brings two people together in a way that is hard to ignore. By moving rapidly from "Hello" to the bedroom, we cheapen the relationship and basically say, "You're not important to me, only convenient." We all crave the closeness we feel after being intimate with someone. Unfortunately, when we try to find a partner solely to satisfy us physically, often what we are really looking for just a way to fill an emotional void. Sex can <u>not</u> make you feel loved. It is that false hope that keeps people feeling unfulfilled even though they may have had many partners. Sex <u>can</u> truly enhance an intimate relationship, but without an emotional connection, sex will just leave you feeling empty and alone.

18) Never present your boss with a problem until you have already thought of a possible solution.

Supervisors have a great deal on their minds and the last thing they need is one more problem to worry about. It is inevitable that the negative feelings they feel when confronted by setbacks will also be mentally associated with you. By the same token, when you immediately outline solutions your supervisor cannot help but associate you with feelings of relief and gratitude. Don't hide problems, but be prepared to provide resolution.

19) Be attentive.

Look the speaker in the eye and think about what he/she is saying, not about what _you_ are going to say next. Active listening is a skill that will greatly enhance your ability to communicate. No one likes the feeling of being disregarded or marginalized. If your side of the conversation could be a paragraph by itself and only slightly relates to what the other person was saying, then you are not communicating. Communication is a two way process. Listen, think, and then respond to what you heard. It is also often helpful to repeat back the other person's points periodically for clarification.

20) Don't drink and drive.

Enough said.

21) Always be working toward a goal.

Do not become complacent or self-satisfied once you have attained a goal. Rather, immediately set and pursue a new goal. In the words of General George S. Patton, US Army Retired, "Fixed fortifications are monuments to the stupidity of man. To be victorious we must constantly advance."

22) Work for your own self-satisfaction,
and not just to please others.

People-pleasers are always destined for disappointment.

23) Know the difference between adventure and simple adversity.

There is a distinct difference. What most people call adventure is really just a healthy dose of adversity. Suffering is not necessary to prove you are having fun. To paraphrase John Schandelmeier, two-time winner of the Yukon Quest; "Only city people and amateurs seek adventure. Adventures are when something goes wrong and you are ill prepared. The point is to go into the wilderness prepared enough and savvy enough that you <u>don't</u> have an adventure."

24) Don't waste your time pursuing fantasies like unicorns, El Dorado, winning the lottery, or attaining the perfect relationship.

Work toward realistic and achievable goals.

25) It is generally not a good idea to play the "Good Samaritan."

No matter how noble your intentions, often even the people you are trying to help will end up testifying against you.

26) Take responsibility for your life.

Do not blame your parents, your boss, the government, or people of a particular ethnic group for problems that you have brought upon yourself.

27) Take the time to plan for the future.

Do not trust to fate or luck. As Earl Nightingale points out, "Luck is what happens when opportunity meets preparedness."

28) Be aware that you may not always receive what you deserve.

Also, know that others may have a different opinion of you and your behavior. So, no matter how painful it may be, in their eyes you may be getting exactly what you deserve.

29) Remember the Chinese proverb, "The enemy of your enemy is not necessarily your friend."

Politics is everywhere today. Do not make the mistake of overlooking someone's personal motives just because you seem to be on the same side. Even if you currently have a common enemy, once that enemy is vanquished your so-called ally may turn on you next.

30) Be careful where you plant your flag.

Think about the political, social and financial consequences of a position before you proclaim to the world where you stand

31) Be wary of people who claim to like everyone and are constantly complimentary.

It is a very common ploy to lull someone into a false sense of security through compliments and praise. We are all susceptible to flattery. It is, however, important to ask why we're being applauded even as we are graciously taking a bow.

32) When you lose at something or feel insulted try to remember that in most cases it's not personal.

Most people are reactionary and don't put much thought into how something will make a person feel before they act or speak out. The way they come across to you may actually have very little to do with your actions. More likely an outburst seemingly is targeted at you but really is based in some totally unrelated frustration in their lives. People often "fly off the handle" simply because of some turmoil that has been simmering just beneath the surface. Be comforted by the fact that more often than not, it's not about you.

33) Forgive others whenever possible.

On those rare occasions when it really was a personal attack: take the moral high ground. Remind yourself that it is internal pain that is causing your attackers to act that way. Again, they probably don't even recognize their own subconscious motivations. A very wise man once said, "Forgive them Father, for they know not what they do."

34) Don't be a "Yes-Man."

Present your honest and open opinion when asked. Of course, be courteous and aware of to whom you are speaking but do not be afraid to disagree or go against the popular opinion. Yes-men are often tolerated, and may even be able to ride the coattails of those they agree with for a while. But eventually, managers find they need someone whose feedback bears listening too. Having their ego stroked only gets them so far, but having quality advisors can really boost their advancement options.

35) Pursue excellence quietly and steadily.

Do not waste energy on confrontations with the base and ignorant members of your peer group. Quality managers are both aware of and constantly on the look out for the team members who actually perform the work as opposed to those who merely take the credit. It is generally not necessary to loudly "blow your own horn." Ensure that others know that the work is yours, but more importantly, quietly persevere in your pursuit of quality. Your supervisor, or more likely, your supervisor's supervisor, will become increasingly aware of who really keeps the ball rolling. Let others spend their time and resources scratching and clawing each other. Don't let yourself get dragged into the drama. As Sun Tsu said in The Art of War, "If you sit by the river long enough, the body of your enemy will float past."

36) Be open minded and accepting of change.

There are often many ways to solve a problem. Be objective and listen to all sides and options before deciding on a course of action. Do not get caught in the trap of fixating on a solution that you are familiar with at the expense of a better, faster, or cheaper fix. "To a man with a hammer, every problem looks like a nail." Don't let this be your motto.

37) Add value every day.

Don't be a member of the vast masses who merely go through the motions each day. Ask yourself daily, "What can I do to make this work better, faster, more efficiently?" Then answer that question and do it! If you constantly strive to add value in everything you do, you will never need to worry about being left behind, laid off, nor excluded.

38) When facing a list of projects, tackle the most difficult one first.

Tough projects can be a little intimidating. The best strategy is to tackle them right away while you are still fresh. Later when you are wearing down you will be finishing up. Then if you have time, you can work on a smaller, easier project with your remaining time and energy without feeling overwhelmed. It is also important to note that tough projects should be faced head on. One sure way to get over the intimidation factor is to just get started. Once you are in motion the project will often simply flow along and no longer seem so daunting.

39) Do not make the mistake of underestimating your opponent.

As the saying goes, big things often come in small packages. If you assume that someone is smarter, stronger, or faster than they actually are and then you far outstrip them anyway, then no harm done. But to assume they are weak, foolish, or slow and find out too late that you were mistaken can be very costly.

40) Make a conscious effort to ensure that your behavior matches your beliefs.

Often individuals will spend time floundering without focus and without achieving their stated goals simply because they have not aligned their actions with their objectives. Spend some time examining what you really believe in deep down and ask yourself if what you do on a day to day basis is moving you toward those beliefs. Goals that are not rooted in core beliefs will either never be fulfilled or will leave you without satisfaction. Similarly, a system of beliefs that is never addressed will lead you to disillusionment and feelings of frustration. Make a written description of your core values and beliefs. Spend time focusing on how you can best address those goals. Perhaps only minor adjustments to your lifestyle are necessary. However, you may find that something as major as a career change or a change in a relationship is in order.

41) It is often better to work with finesse and subtlety than to force an issue.

Practice patience and versatility whenever possible. Being blunt or aggressive will often as not make someone dig in their heels and resist your efforts. It is the height of management skill to get someone to do something that they don't want to do, and to make them think that it was their idea to do it.

42) Be aware that this is the "Information Age."

To be successful it is not always necessary to be the brightest, nor the fastest. Often it is more important that you simply have all the facts. It is especially valuable to have more information than your opponents have. Take the time to research a situation thoroughly before you act. At the very least, it will keep you from blundering into a trap. At best, it will enable you to make wise, farsighted decisions and ensure that you are prepared for all outcomes. No one makes good decisions 100% of the time, but the more informed you are, the more you can minimize the damage from poor decisions and the faster you can change course when necessary.

43) Avoid excessive television watching.

The average adult in the United States watches 6 hours of television a day. The average NFL football game is nearly three hours long! Some recreational television can help you relax of course, but if you find yourself "channel surfing" it's a sure sign that your brain needs more stimulation. Get up and do something productive. Those projects that you have been putting off that we discussed earlier might be knocked out fairly quickly if you were to spend your 6 hours of television time working on them.

44) Pause for a few seconds and think about what you are going to say before you open your mouth and say it.

This allows you to at least give the impression that you are a thoughtful and wise individual. Also, even if you have already made your decision, people, especially subordinates, will more readily accept your point of view if you seem to have thoroughly considered theirs.

45) Do not rely on the word of so-called "experts."

Don't accept arguments at face value, but think about their origins. Also, try not to focus on what people say so much as on why they are saying it. As I have said before, everyone has an agenda. Put some thought into why someone feels the way they do before you allow yourself to be swayed to their point of view. Often, people do not even realize they are selectively omitting facts or skewing an argument. They may have so much invested emotionally that they refuse to even consider the opposing viewpoint. One sure way to make a person invent reasons why they are right is to offer a logical reason why they are wrong,

46) Smile, even when you talk on the telephone and you are alone in the room.

People can tell when you are being friendly even when they can't see you. Be the type of person who engenders good will. Smiling changes the whole tone of the conversation. It is a known fact that you can change your mood by lying to your body. The next time you feel blue or angry try forcing yourself to smile for three or four minutes straight. It will undoubtedly brighten your spirits and make you less irritable. Other people will also react positively to your smile and that will make you feel better too.

47) Remember that just because you read something or heard someone say it on the television that does not necessarily mean it is true.

Truth in media is, unfortunately, a thing of the past. Media personalities are allowed to print or say whatever they like as long as they do not intend to do harm. You may have heard of the "absence of malice" stipulation in the laws governing mass media. They are also allowed, and often do, present opinion pieces as factual stories or "news." Think for yourself. Why should someone automatically be assumed to be a credible source of information just because they are seen or read by millions of people? Also, we do not know that their source of information was reliable. Many "news" reporters have been duped by someone with an axe to grind.

48) Be constantly on the alert for conclusions based upon false assumptions or faulty logic.

So much of today's rhetoric surrounding political and social issues is based upon illogic and false premises. A traffic school instructor of mine once stated, "Most people who have been in an accident think that overall they are good drivers. Jane thinks that she is a good driver, so she is probably going to get into an accident." When you stop and think about this statement, you may realize that it is the same as saying, "All alligators are green. This is green. Therefore, it must be an alligator." This is, of course, ridiculous. Be critical in your belief system. Think about the facts and come to your own conclusions. Do not be a sheep following the herd. The mob mentality can only lead you to disillusionment.

49) Be careful whom you associate yourself with.

Avoid the loud and aggressive. Also, do not associate more than in a passing fashion with the dishonest or deceitful. Others will judge you by the company you keep. It is also likely that the more often you are exposed to ungentlemanly behavior the less out of line it will seem. Eventually, you will act and speak like those you have surrounded yourself with.

50) Shower, shave, and dress nicely regardless of your plan for the day.

Even on the days when you sleep late and plan only to relax around the house, you never know when someone might just drop by. You may also find it necessary to make a "quick" trip to the market. Though you may have been in the store a dozen times in a suit, people will remember the one time you went in looking slovenly.

51) Donate time or money to a charitable cause on a regular basis.

Have you ever looked back over your life or at the lives of people you have known for many years and thought about how things might have turned out quite differently? If you were a rowdy "tough guy" in school, what stroke of good fortune kept you alive and out of prison when others around you were not so lucky? Many people consider themselves to have succeeded because of their own hard work and perseverance, and certainly there is much truth to this. But accidents and poor judgment have ended many a career and/or life. Be thankful for what you have attained and give back to those whose life didn't turn out so well. Recognize that, "It could have been you." Humility and generosity go hand in hand. Help others and you will feel better about yourself and less inclined toward arrogance.

52) Maintain and categorize your wardrobe.

Discard all clothing with holes or stains. Or, at the very least, set them aside for painting, etc. Tee shirts and sweatpants are for exercising, not for everyday wear. Look sharp whenever possible. People will treat you with more respect and you will get better service if you take pride in your appearance. Try this experiment. Go into a car dealership in a suit and start looking at the floor models. Notice how fast a salesman comes to assist you. The next day, go into a different dealership wearing a Polo shirt and slacks. Again take note of the response time. On the third day, visit yet another dealership wearing blue jeans and a tee shirt. The results may surprise you.

53) Develop at least one hobby that is just for you.

Make it something that you do just for fun. Learn to play an instrument. Play racquetball. Collect stamps or baseball cards. Get season tickets to the theater. Recreation is what releases anxiety. It is very important to spend time not thinking about the stressors in your life. High blood pressure is rampant in this country and much good can come from relaxing and focusing on something that gives you pleasure. Forget about work and family life for a while, and periodically engage in something that makes you smile.

54) Refer to individuals by name whenever possible, especially in their presence.

Try to avoid pronouns like he and she in your speech. If you are in a group of three or more and you say something to one person about another in the group, the person being referred to may feel alienated and/or marginalized if you don't use his/her proper name.

E/G To Bill about Mary:

1) I disagree with her.

2) I don't think Mary is right.

In the first example Mary may feel impersonalized, or that she has been cut out of the conversation. A good team builder is always looking for ways to make others feel included

55) Develop clean oral habits.

Avoid smoking, chewing gum, or spitting. Brush your teeth and use mouthwash. Carry breath mints for emergencies. Sometimes a cough or sneeze is unavoidable and in those cases cover your mouth. Do not take overly large bites of food and remember that chewing is strictly a "mouth-closed" activity. These things may seem like simple good manners, but they are often overlooked. You would be surprised to know what people think when they are made painfully aware of your poor oral hygiene and health.

56) Never loan money to a friend unless you can afford to lose one or both of them.

Generosity is a wonderful trait to have and who better to benefit than your closest friends. Be aware however, that money can have a corrupting influence even upon the strongest wills. The recipient of your loan may not actively try to fleece you, but may simply view you as the least likely of his creditors to get nasty if he doesn't pay on schedule. Unfortunately, this can go on for quite some time and is often the death knell of a relationship.

57) Do not share details of your social life with family members; especially parents.

At best, their advice will be tainted by their feelings about you and hardly objective. At worst, you will only complain to them about the things your significant other or spouse does that annoy you and not mention those things that please you. This will give your family a very jaded and negative picture of them and will affect the way they are treated at family gatherings. It is rarely necessary to choose between your family and your partner, but recognize that they have different views of who you are and will not likely agree on how you should live.

58) Carry paper and a pen with you at all times.

Don't rely solely on your memory for important notes, appointment reminders, and telephone numbers. A pen and paper can be small and unobtrusive and yet are often needed. Jot down your thoughts and notes on conversations. Keep a daily planner with a consolidation of these notes and a schedule for the coming days. Being organized is a learned behavior. Start by keeping track of the important points that you come across during the day. Always be prepared to write down a quick note.

59) Do not be afraid to make mistakes,

Be bold and confident. It is a known fact that most millionaires have had at least one business or personal bankruptcy and/or business failure. Many have had several. Only by taking risks can you hope to accomplish great things. "He who hesitates is lost."

60) Join a professional or fraternal organization.

Attend meetings and functions as often as possible. Everyone needs a forum where they feel comfortable and where they are allowed to be themselves. Fraternal organizations such as Kiwanis, The Masonic Order, Elk, Moose, and Eagles, to name a few, will allow you to make friends with similar minded people and they often sponsor community or charitable events that will give you the opportunity to contribute something back to the world around you.

61) Listen to the gist of the words,
      not only the words.

Many people today are masters of deception and misdirection. When in a heated discussion or when asking pointed questions, be sure you are aware of the implications and meaning of your subjects replies. Do not be fooled by a similarity in topic that does not address the question at hand. For example: Question: "Do you think that the policeman used excessive force?" Answer: "I think that we have an obligation to support our law enforcement personnel whenever possible." You may or may not agree with this statement but it did not address the question that was asked.

62) Avoid using slurs and generalities.

Referring to someone as a bimbo, idiot, jerk, or worse may make you feel better, but in the eyes of others it will make you look like an emotion driven boor. Try to remain calm and objective and do not make blanket judgments about people. Additionally, if you stop and think about individuals you know personally, you will realize that no two are alike so it is impossible to believe that all members of a particular race or nationality have the same negative characteristics. The bottom line is that making disparaging comments about others is unprofessional and they are rarely completely accurate.

63) There are two things that everyone wants to know about you and that should never be discussed with anyone outside your immediate family: how much money you make and the details of your sex life.

Absolutely no good can come from discussions with the general populous on these two subjects. At the very least, knowledge of your salary level and sexual habits can only serve to change the way others look at you. At worst, speculation on these topics will lead to discord, resentment, and animosity.

64) Don't simply exist, but truly <u>live</u> your life.

Savor every moment. Take time to look around and see the beauty that is everywhere. Flowers, children, animals, sunshine, and rainbows all are reminders that this life is worth living. If you find yourself bored then try something out of the ordinary. A new ethnic restaurant or foreign film can be a great wake up call. Appreciate the love and excitement of life's little adventures and try not to get bogged down in the difficulties of day-to-day routine.

65) Keep a daily record of your life.

A daily planner is a great tool for this. Before bed make a quick note of the day's events including impressions and important names and numbers. Some planner systems allow for topic headings as well, which will aid in finding the notes you are looking for later. Keeping this diary will clarify your thoughts and help you focus upon possible solutions to problems.

66) It is often easier to beg for forgiveness than to ask for permission.

Some people in supervisory positions will say "no" simply for the sake of exercising their power. If you think you are right and the consequences of being wrong are not monumental, then take the chance and make a decision. Be a man of action.

67) Never try to teach a pig to sing. It wastes your time, and annoys the pig.

There are those among us who do not have the inclination or perhaps the mental capacity to appreciate the finer things in life. This does not mean some people are better than others, nor more important. It simply means that we have differing priorities. A Nascar fan may not appreciate a symphony orchestra. But equally a connoisseur of fine art may not see the beauty in a well designed 1.5 horsepower, fourteen inch blade, worm drive, circular saw. Do not waste time trying to win over converts to your hobbies and way of thinking. Revel in your own pursuits and let others remain where they are.

68) It is enough just to know.

It is not necessary to convince the world that you are right if in fact you are. Be content with that knowledge. A sure sign of how certain someone is of their position or faith is the vigor with which they try and convert you to their way of thinking. Simply ask yourself, "Which one of us is he trying to convince, me or himself?"

69) You cannot say the wrong thing to the right person, nor the right thing to the wrong person.

If someone is ready to hear what you have to say, that is, receptive to considering your point of view, then you need not work very hard to try and convince him or her. Conversely, if a person has already made up their mind that you have nothing important to share, then no amount of arguing will bring them around.

70) Follow the money.

Sadly, a huge motivator in today's American society is greed and avarice. When seeking to find out why something is happening, always ask yourself who stands to benefit financially from the situation. It may not be obvious, but a little research will often bring out some very interesting facts about funding and potential profits.

71) Make a list of what excites you and what worries you.

This is a good exercise to do at least weekly. Putting your concerns and desires on paper serves to focus your attention and helps you determine what should be done. An interesting exercise is to have each member of the family make this list of desires and worries each holiday season and, without sharing them, put them away with the holiday decorations for a few years. Years later the family will no doubt be very amused by what seemed so important not so long ago.

72) Those also serve who stand and wait.   Milton

It is not only those in the line of fire who provide for our well being. Remember the "little people" who provide so much to our daily lives. This is perhaps not exactly what Milton was trying to say, but nonetheless whether quietly supporting the team on the home front, or actively carrying out orders, everyone has an important piece of the overall plan to carry out. Cooks, cleaners, clerks etc. all play a vital, if unexciting, roll in the battle. Mothers especially are today's unsung heroes, keeping everything in order without asking for much in return. Try to be grateful and appreciative of everyone's contribution.

73) If it's not broken don't fix it.

The surest way to render something inoperable is to try to make ad hoc improvements to it. "I'll just make a minor adjustment and this will work so much better!" Famous last words. If it is your profession or area of expertise then fine. If not, leave well enough alone or call for assistance from people who know how to do it right the first time.

74) Put the wood <u>on</u> the fire, not <u>in</u> the fire.

Boy Scout lore? Possibly, but a good point nonetheless. To build a successful project, like a fire, the fuel must be added a little at a time in a logical, orderly fashion. Too much or in the wrong place and the project/fire will smother and collapse. Be precise. Pick your additions carefully and base them upon your goals not upon a desire for instant heat/gratification. You want the fire to last and create a bed of coals for the night. Similarly, a project must be nurtured to take on its own life and become successful. Plan the fire. Anticipate possible setbacks and take steps to avoid them. For example, don't build your fire under a snow laden tree.

75) Its not gossip if it's true?!

A ridiculous statement if ever I've heard one. Discussing other people's personal lives is irresponsible and can have quite hurtful consequences. Keep idle gossip to a minimum. If the person you're talking to is not directly involved in the situation then consider yourself to be gossiping. Whether you're retelling true events or speculating, either way nothing good can come of it.

76) A leopard cannot change its spots.

Be wary of those who have proven themselves to be unreliable or untrustworthy and now claim to have changed their ways. Habits, especially bad ones, are hard to break and without a "life-changing-event" most people are neither willing nor able to make the effort.

A young Native American was trudging through the winter snow one morning when he happened upon a rattlesnake shivering on a rock. "Please, take me home and warm me or will freeze to death," said the rattlesnake. "Oh no," replied the boy, "If I pick you up you will bite me and then I will be the one to die." "I promise not to bite you if you will help me," pleaded the snake. So the young brave picked up the rattlesnake and carried it home to his lodge. There he laid it near the fire, and placed bowls of meat and water before it. After a while the boy reached down to remove the empty bowls and the snake struck and buried his fangs deep in the boy's arm. The brave jumped back in surprise and pain and exclaimed, "You said that if I would help you that you would not bite me!" The rattlesnake replied with an evil grin, "You knew what I was."

77) Nothing is free in life except the cheese in the trap.

A price must always be paid for beneficial things. If you can accept this fact then you will not be taken in by one of the thousands of charlatans and con men in the world. If it seems to good to be true, then it probably is, as the saying goes. Do your homework. Check references and trade associations. The Better Business Bureau and the Federal Trade Commission both maintain extensive records of complaints and instances of false advertising.

78) Short cuts make for long delays.

This is not to say that you should always stick to the beaten path, just make sure you know where you're going and how to get there efficiently. Trying new shortcuts when you are in a hurry more often than not will make you later than if you had stayed on the main road. Seek out shortcuts when you have spare time. Then you have a sure thing to work with when you are rushed

79) Don't burn your bridges.

If something doesn't work out for you, bow out gracefully and try not to offend anyone in the process. People will remember you and your work only if they don't remember that you acted inappropriately on your last trip out the door. Opportunities have a way of coming full circle. If they pass you by once and you don't come unglued then you may get another chance.

80) When your opponent is on the ropes and retreating, pursue him and finish him off.

Do not look for trouble, but if someone pushes you into a corner and attacks you, then take no prisoners. A wounded adversary will slink away and nurture a grudge, plotting and scheming about his future revenge. When you have him reeling, pounce on him and make sure he knows that he should seek out easier prey next time.

81) Know that bullies are always cowards.

Those who pick on the weak or less fortunate are invariably scared and insecure inside. Stand up for yourself. If you show determination and courage or can get in at least one painful blow, more often than not a bully will back down. Persistence in a fight is difficult to maintain without inner courage, and bullies have none.

82) Someone has to draw first blood.

Don't be afraid to let it be you. We've all been there; afraid to make a move, unsure of the fallout. As young boys how many of us sat next to a girl and didn't dare to put our arm around her shoulder for fear of being rebuffed when in reality she was wishing we would do it too? Be brave in these situations. Even though you may feel emotionally vulnerable, try to remember that if it doesn't work out, you are really no worse off than you were when you started. In fact, you're better off knowing where you stand. Take a chance. You might be pleasantly surprised.

83) Expand your vocabulary.

According to a Harvard research study the best indicator of the level to which a supervisor will rise is his or her depth of vocabulary. In short, front line supervisors can express themselves more fully than their subordinates, managers more fully than supervisors, executives more fully than managers, etc. Work on your vocabulary daily. Read widely and read challenging material. The average newspaper is written at a seventh grade reading level. Do not rely on that medium alone. Merriam Webster publishes a terrific daily vocabulary builder text, which I highly recommend. The better you can make yourself understood the higher you will rise in any organization.

84) Stay in school as long as possible.

The key to prospering in today's world is education. Further, the younger you are the easier it is to pursue an education. Sacrifice and work hard in school as long as you can. Most well paying jobs are only available to those with degrees. You can't even get into the military without a High School diploma or GED. Put in the time and effort now and you will have many more options later in life

85) Pay attention to your health.

Like it or not you will only get one body for this lifetime. If you do not pay attention to maintenance issues it will not last as long as you need it to. Exercise, get enough rest and relaxation, and eat nutritious food. Drug use, excessive alcohol consumption, or a sedentary lifestyle will have the net effect of shortening your life. No preaching here, just a fact to think about.

86) Not everything is an anecdote.

There are few things more annoying than an over-talkative person who wants to relate every minute detail of their lives. Admittedly, some humorous incidents or certain quotes or experiences from children's lives bear repeating and make for interesting conversation, but keep in mind what you find amusing your audience may find dull. Also, be aware of the tendency most people have toward conversational one-upmanship. That is, to try to top the last story with a better one. This inevitably leads to exaggeration and feelings of resentment. Let others have the limelight in equal turn. There are no extra points given for monopolizing the conversation.

87) Trust your intuition.

Our brains are wonderful and complex machines capable of processing information even when we are not consciously aware of it. You may not be able to put you finger on why you think something is a good or bad idea but your subconscious may be reminding you of something you know or heard but aren't remembering. Listen to that little voice. It's usually right.

88) There are neither accidents nor coincidences in life.

It is a sometimes-frightening truth that everything happens for a reason. We often may not understand why or even feel unfairly victimized, but we can be comforted by the knowledge that there is purpose in the universe.

89) What you think most about, you will become.

I am a big believer in the philosophy that we each create our own reality. If you focus on something enough, it will happen. This is not really so much a metaphysical view, as it is psychological. For instance, if you constantly read about archeology, you will become more attuned to opportunities to go on archeological digs and expeditions. Similarly, if you spend all of your time studying martial arts you will seek out real life situations in which to practice them, perhaps with unintended results.

90) Don't take anything for granted.

Life is constantly changing and evolving. Be prepared for all possible outcomes. Think about insurance and safety in advance. No one ever thinks bad things will happen to them, and it is a sure thing that most people try not to think about death, although it will take each of us eventually. Perhaps you will live a charmed life, but you would be well served by planning for all contingencies. Carry a first-aid kit in your car. Buy life insurance. Don't worry yourself unnecessarily, just plan ahead.

91) If you don't like your life then change it!

Make a commitment right now to take personal responsibility for your life. No one has more at stake than you do in your future. Don't cop out as so many do and settle for mediocrity and a constant state of whining and complaining about how unfair life is. Take steps to improve your condition. Learn, grow, and expand your knowledge and experience. Don't be afraid to take a chance. Put your own house in order, and branch out and make a change when necessary. You will soon leave the complainers behind.

92) Avoid aggressive belligerent people.

These people seem to create a wave of hate and discontentment in their world. Angry, hateful people will infect those around them with similar feelings. Avoid them at all cost.

93) Don't bet on the queen of diamonds; always bet on the queen of hearts.

It's the age-old question of love vs. money. Believe me, if given the choice, always opt for love. Riches are fleeting, and a woman solely attracted to, or consumed with desire for, wealth will do her best to dominate you and will constantly push you to provide more. A woman who is willing to love you as you are will offer a much more fulfilling relationship when you do become successful, and if it takes a little longer than anticipated to reach your goals then you will also be happier along the way.

94) The world belongs to the diligent and persistent.

Practice, practice, practice! Remember that nobody ever started out doing something like an expert. Everything takes persistence and diligent attention to master. Put in the time it takes to learn and grow. Often the better you become at something the more fun it is as well

95) Others will judge you by your personal appearance. Goatees, tattoos, and body piercings may be fun but may be intimidating to some.

I am not making a value judgment here, only an observation. Societal leaders and captains of industry look much the same today as they did 50, 100 and even 150 years ago, clothes not withstanding. They are clean cut and conservative in appearance. People can't help but have more confidence in those who look professional and seem to take pride in their personal appearance.

96) Don't forget where you are.

The number one cause of accidents is people not paying attention to their surroundings. We get caught up in the moment and forget where we are. We lean over to pick something up or play with the radio while hurtling down the highway. We concentrate so much on the chore at hand that we step backward off a ladder. Etc. Be aware of the inherent hazards in what you are doing. Have respect for your situation and don't focus so completely that you lose sight of possible dangers.

97) If you wouldn't want anyone to know, then don't do it.

A good test question might be, "Does this action require privacy or secrecy?" We all have personal lives that we don't normally share with outsiders and these things fall under the heading of privacy. Secrecy, however, is usually only required when something is illegal, immoral or such a departure from our normal way of life that we would be mortified if our family and friends found out. Avoid actions that call for secrecy.

98) Base decisions upon ethical and moral convictions not upon possible outcomes.

It is a sad truth that while a hundred years ago people were mainly deterred from crime by a sense of right and wrong, today the main deterrent is fear of punishment. The prevailing thought in today's society is "If you can get away with it, go for it!" People routinely cheat on their taxes, pirate cable television signals and park in the handicapped zone. Try to maintain a high level of moral and ethical standards in all your decision-making. Petty transgressions breed a false sense of security which leads to more serious offences with more drastic consequences. Be honest and moral in all aspects of your life,

99) As important as who you are and what you can do is who you know.

With the exception of military service, every job I've ever held I've gotten by knowing someone or being recommended by a friend or colleague. Networking can be an invaluable tool in furthering your career. Take the time to get to know people and find out more about them. Often you will have something in common that you can expand into a friendship. Be friendly and outgoing toward everyone you meet. You never know who is going to remember you and offer you a position.

100) Do not rely on books like this one to give you all of your answers.

There is no substitute for experience. Use this manual as a guide to help you avoid common mistakes but recognize that you will find your own truth and answers simply by living your life.

www.ingramcontent.com/pod-product-compliance
Lightning Source LLC
Chambersburg PA
CBHW071723040426
42446CB00011B/2193